Lill's
Travels

IN SANTA CLAUS LAND

AND OTHER
STORIES

ELLIS TOWNE, SOPHIE MAY
AND ELLA FARMAN

[ZHINGOORA BOOKS]

LILL'S TRAVELS IN SANTA CLAUS LAND.

EFFIE had been playing with her dolls one cold December morning, and Lill had been reading, until both were tired. But it stormed too hard to go out, and, as Mrs. Pelerine had said they need not do anything for two hours, their little jaws might have been dislocated by yawning before they would as much as pick up a pin. Presently Lill said, "Effie, shall I tell you a story."

"O yes! do!" said Effie, and she climbed up by Lill in the large rocking-chair in front of the grate. She kept very still, for she knew Lill's stories were not to be interrupted by a sound, or even a motion. The first thing Lill did was to fix her eyes on the fire, and rock backward and forward quite hard for a little while, and then she said, "Now I am going to tell you about my *thought travels*, and they are apt to be a little queerer, but O! ever so much nicer, than the other kind!"

As Lill's stories usually had a formal introduction she began: "Once upon a time, when I was taking a walk through the great field beyond the orchard, I went way on, 'round where the path turns behind the hill. And after I had walked a little way, I came to a high wall—built right up into the sky. At first I thought I had discovered the 'ends of the earth,' or perhaps I had somehow come to the great wall of China. But after walking a long way I came to a large gate, and over it was printed in beautiful gold letters, 'SANTA CLAUS LAND,' and the letters were large enough for a baby to read!"

How large that might be Lill did not stop to explain.

"But the gate was shut tight," she continued, "and though I knocked and knocked and knocked, as hard as I could, nobody came to open it. I was dreadfully disappointed, because I felt as if Santa Claus must live here all of the year except when he went out to pay Christmas visits, and it would be so lovely to see him in his own home, you know. But what was I to do? The gate was entirely too high to climb over, and there wasn't even a crack to peek through!"

Here Lill paused, and Effie drew a long breath, and looked greatly disappointed. Then Lill went on:

"But you see, as I was poking about, I pressed a bell-spring, and in a moment—jingle, jingle, jingle, the bells went ringing far and near, with such a merry sound as was never heard before. While they were still ringing the gate slowly opened and I walked in. I didn't even stop to inquire if Santa Claus was at home, for I forgot all about myself and my manners, it was so lovely. First there was a small paved square like a court; it was surrounded by rows and rows of dark green trees, with several avenues opening between them.

"In the centre of the court was a beautiful marble fountain, with streams of sugar plums and bon-bons tumbling out of it. Funny-looking little men were filling cornucopias at the fountain, and pretty little barefoot children, with chubby hands and dimpled shoulders, took them as soon as they were filled, and ran off with them. They were all too much occupied to speak to me, but as I came up to the fountain one of the funny little fellows gave me a cornucopia, and I marched on with the babies.

"We went down one of the avenues, which would have been very dark only it was splendidly lighted up with Christmas candles. I saw the babies were slyly eating a candy or two, so I tasted mine, and they were delicious— the real Christmas kind. After we had gone a little way, the trees were smaller and not so close together, and here there were other funny little fellows who were climbing up on ladders and tying toys and bon-bons to the trees. The children stopped and delivered their packages, but I walked on, for there was something in the distance that I was curious to see. I could see that it was a large garden, that looked as if it might be well cared for, and had many things growing in it. But even in the distance it didn't look natural, and when I reached it I found it was a very uncommon kind of a garden indeed. I could scarcely believe my eyes, but there were dolls and donkeys and drays and cars and croquet coming up in long, straight rows, and ever so many other things beside. In one place the wooden dolls had only just started; their funny little heads were just above ground, and I thought they looked very much surprised at their surroundings. Farther on were china dolls, that looked quite grown up, and I suppose were ready to pull; and a gardener was hoeing a row of soldiers that didn't look in a very healthy condition, or as if they had done very well.

"The gardener looked familiar, I thought, and as I approached him he stopped work and, leaning on his hoe he said, 'How do you do, Lilian? I am very glad to see you.'

"The moment he raised his face I knew it was Santa Claus, for he looked exactly like the portrait we have of him. You can easily believe I was glad then! I ran and put both of my hands in his, fairly shouting that I was so glad to find him.

"He laughed and said:

"'Why, I am generally to be found here or hereabouts, for I work in the grounds every day.'

"And I laughed too, because his laugh sounded so funny; like the brook going over stones, and the wind up in the trees. Two or three times, when I thought he had done he would burst out again, laughing the vowels in this way: 'Ha, ha, ha, ha! He, he, he, he, he! Hi, hi, hi, hi, hi! Ho, ho, ho, h-o-oo!'"

Lill did it very well, and Effie laughed till the tears came to her eyes; and she could quite believe Lill when she said, "It grew to be so funny that I couldn't stand, but fell over into one of the little chairs that were growing in a bed just beyond the soldiers.

"When Santa Claus saw that he stopped suddenly, saying:

"'There, that will do. I take a hearty laugh every day, for the sake of digestion.'

"Then he added, in a whisper, 'That is the reason I live so long and don't grow old. I've been the same age ever since the chroniclers began to take notes, and those who are best able to judge think I'll continue to be this way for about one thousand eight hundred and seventy-six years longer,—they probably took a new observation at the Centennial, and they know exactly.'

"I was greatly delighted to hear this, and I told him so. He nodded and winked and said it was 'all right,' and then asked if I'd like to see the place. I said I would, so he threw down the hoe with a sigh, saying, 'I don't believe I shall have more than half a crop of soldiers this season. They came up well, but the arms and legs seem to be weak. When I get to town I'll have to send out some girls with glue pots, to stick them fast.'

"The town was at some distance, and our path took us by flower-beds where some exquisite little toys were growing, and a hot-bed where new varieties were being prop—*propagated*. Pretty soon we came to a plantation of young trees, with rattles, and rubber balls, and ivory rings growing on the branches, and as we went past they rang and bounded about in the merriest sort of a way.

"'There's a nice growth,' said Santa Claus, and it *was* a nice growth for babies; but just beyond I saw something so perfectly splendid that I didn't care about the plantation."

"Well," said Lill impressively, seeing that Effie was sufficiently expectant, "It was a lovely grove. The trees were large, with long droopingbranches, and the branches were just loaded with dolls' clothes. There were elegant silk dresses, with lovely sashes of every color—"

Just here Effie couldn't help saying "O!" for she had a weakness for sashes.

Lill looked stern, and put a warning hand over her mouth, and went on.

"There was everything that the most fashionable doll could want, growing in the greatest profusion. Some of the clothes had fallen, and there were funny-looking girls picking them up, and packing them in trunks and boxes. 'These are all ripe,' said Santa Claus, stopping to shake a tree, and the clothes came tumbling down so fast that the workers were busier than ever. The grove was on a hill, so that we had a beautiful view of the country. First there was a park filled with reindeer, and beyond that was the town, and at one side a large farm-yard filled with animals of all sorts.

"But as Santa Claus seemed in a hurry I did not stop long to look. Our path led through the park, and we stopped to call 'Prancer' and 'Dancer' and 'Donder' and 'Blitzen,' and Santa Claus fed them with lumps of sugar from his pocket. He pointed out 'Comet' and 'Cupid' in a distant part of the park; 'Dasher' and 'Vixen' were nowhere to be seen.

"Here I found most of the houses were Swiss cottages, but there were some fine churches and public buildings, all of beautifully illustrated building blocks, and we stopped for a moment at a long depot, in which a locomotive was just *smashing up*.

"Santa Claus' house stood in the middle of the town. It was an old-fashioned looking house, very broad and low, with an enormous chimney. There was a wide step in front of the door, shaded by a fig-tree and grape-vine, and morning-glories and scarlet beans clambered by the side of the latticed windows; and there were great round rose-bushes, with great, round roses, on either side of the walk leading to the door."

"O! it must have smelled like a party," said Effie, and then subsided, as she remembered that she was interrupting.

"Inside, the house was just cozy and comfortable, a real grandfatherly sort of a place. A big chair was drawn up in front of the window, and a big book was open on a table in front of the chair. A great pack half made up was on the floor, and Santa Claus stopped to add a few things from his pocket. Then he went to the kitchen, and brought me a lunch of milk and strawberries and cookies, for he said I must be tired after my long walk.

"After I had rested a little while, he said if I liked I might go with him to the observatory. But just as we were starting a funny little fellow stopped at the door with a wheelbarrow full of boxes of dishes. After Santa Claus had taken the boxes out and put them in the pack he said slowly,—

"'Let me see!'

"He laid his finger beside his nose as he said it, and looked at me attentively, as if I were a sum in addition, and he was adding me up. I guess I must have come out right, for he looked satisfied, and said I'd better go to the mine first, and then join him in the observatory. Now I am afraid he was not exactly polite not to go with me himself," added Lill, gravely, "but then he apologized by saying he had some work to do. So I followed the little fellow with the wheelbarrow, and we soon came to what looked like the entrance of a cave, but I suppose it was the mine. Ifollowed my guide to the interior without stopping to look at the boxes and piles of dishes outside. Here I found other funny little people, busily at work with picks and shovels, taking out wooden dishes from the bottom of the cave, and china and glass from the top and sides, for the dishes hung down just like stalactites in Mammoth Cave."

Here Lill opened the book she had been reading, and showed Effie a picture of the stalactites.

"It was so curious and so pretty that I should have remained longer," said Lill, "only I remembered the observatory and Santa Claus.

"When I went outside I heard his voice calling out, 'Lilian! Lilian!' It sounded a great way off, and yet somehow it seemed to fill the air just as the wind does. I only had to look for a moment, for very near by was a high tower. I wonder I did not see it before; but in these queer countries you are sure to see something new every time you look about. Santa Claus was standing up at a window near the top, and I ran to the entrance and commenced climbing the stairs. It was a long journey, and I was quite out of breath when I came to the end of it. But here there was such a cozy, luxurious little room, full of stuffed chairs and lounges, bird cages and flowers in the windows, and pictures on the wall, that it was delightful to rest. There was a lady sitting by a golden desk, writing in a large book, and Santa Claus was looking through a great telescope, and every once in a while he stopped and put his ear to a large speaking-tube. While I was resting he went on with his observations.

"Presently he said to the lady, 'Put down a good mark for Sarah Buttermilk. I see she is trying to conquer her quick temper.'

"'Two bad ones for Isaac Clappertongue; he'll drive his mother to the insane asylum yet.'

"'Bad ones all around for the Crossley children,—they quarrel too much.'

"'A good one for Harry and Alice Pleasure, they are quick to mind.'

"'And give Ruth Olive ten, for she is a peacemaker.'"

Just then he happened to look at me and saw I was rested, so he politely asked what I thought of the country. I said it was magnificent. He said he was sorry I didn't stop in the green-house, where he had wax dolls and other delicate things growing. I was very sorry about that, and then I said I thought he must be very happy to own so many delightful things.

"'Of course I'm happy,' said Santa Claus, and then he sighed. 'But it is an awful responsibility to reward so many children according to their deserts. For

I take these observations every day, and I know who is good and who is bad.'

"I was glad he told me about this, and now, if he would only tell me what time of day he took the observations, I would have obtained really valuable information. So I stood up and made my best courtesy and said,—

"'Please, sir, would you tell me what time of day you usually look?'

"'O,' he answered, carelessly, 'any time from seven in the morning till ten at night. I am not a bit particular about time. I often go without my own meals in order to make a record of table manners. For instance: last evening I saw you turn your spoon over in your mouth, and that's very unmannerly for a girl nearly fourteen.'

"'O, I didn't know *you* were looking,' said I, very much ashamed; 'and I'll never do it again,' I promised.

"Then he said I might look through the telescope, and I looked right down into our house. There was mother very busy and very tired, and all of the children teasing. It was queer, for I was there, too, and the *bad-est* of any. Pretty soon I ran to a quiet corner with a book, and in a few minutes mamma had to leave her work and call, 'Lilian, Lilian, it's time for you to practise.'

"'Yes, mamma,' I answered, 'I'll come right away.'

"As soon as I said this Santa Claus whistled for 'Comet' and 'Cupid,' and they came tearing up the tower. He put me in a tiny sleigh, and away we went, over great snow-banks of clouds, and before I had time to think I was landed in the big chair, and mamma was calling 'Lilian, Lilian, it's time for you to practise,' just as she is doing now, and I must go."

So Lill answered, "Yes, mamma," and ran to the piano.

Effie sank back in the chair to think. She wished Lill had found out how many black marks she had, and whether that lady was Mrs. Santa Claus—and had, in fact, obtained more accurate information about many things.

But when she asked about some of them afterwards, Lill said she didn't know, for the next time she had traveled in that direction she foundSANTA CLAUS LAND had moved.

WHAT HAPPENED TO KATHIE AND LU.

IT was a very great misfortune, and it must have been a sad affliction to the friends of the two children, for both were once pretty and charming.

It came about in this way.

Little Winnie Tennyson—she wasn't the daughter of Mr. Alfred Tennyson, the poet-laureate of England, but *was* as sweet as any one of that gentleman's poems—had been to the city; and she had brought home so many wondrous improvements that her two little bosom friends, Lu Medway and Kathie Dysart, were almost struck dumb to behold and to hear what Winnie said and what Winnie had.

For one thing, there were some wooden blocks, all fluted and grooved, and Winnie could heat these blocks in the oven, and wet her hair, and lay it between them, and O! how satin-smooth the waves would be,—hair-pin-crimps and braid-crimps were nothing to this new and scientific way.

Winnie also made it a matter of pride to display her overskirts. These were arranged with ever so many tapes on the inside, and would readily tie up into the most ravishing bunches and puffs—

how Lu and Kathie, wee-est mites of women though they were, did envy Winnie her tapes! Their mammas didn't know how to loop a dress— witness their little skirts pinned back into what Kathie called a "wopse."

She also had brought some tiny parlor skates, and, withal, many airs and graces which her two young-lady aunties had taught her, among others a funny little new accent on some of her words,—the word "pretty" in particular. And, last of all, she had been taught to dance!

"And I can show *you*," Winnie said, eagerly, "'cause it goes by 'steps,' and uncle says I take them as pr-i-tty as Cousin Lily."

Now, in Connaut, little girls don't dance—not *nice* little girls, nor nice big girls either, for that matter.

The dimpled mouths opened in astonishment. "That is wicked, Winnie Ten'son, don't you know?"

"O, but 'tisn't," said Winnie. "My aunties dance, and their mamma, my grandmamma, was at the party once."

"We shall tell our mothers," said Lu. "I'll bet you've come home a proud, wicked girl, and you want us to be as bad as you are."

"WINNIE ALREADY HAD HER CLASS
BEFORE HER."

Now Winnie was only six years old, about the same age as her virtuous friends, and she didn't look very wicked. She had pink cheeks, and blue eyes, and dimples. She stood gazing at her accusers, first at one and then at the other.

"Luie," said Kathie, gravely, "we mustn't call Winnie wicked till we ask our mothers if she is."

"No, I don't think I would," said Mrs. Tennyson, looking up from her sewing, her cheek flushing at the sight of tears in her little Winnie's gentle eyes.

On the way home, they chanced to see their own minister walking along. Lu stopped short. "Kathie," said she, "I know it's awful wicked now, or else we never should have met the minister right here. I'm just going to tell him about Winnie."

She went up to him, Kathie following shyly.

"Mr. Goodhue, Winnie Ten'son is a nawful wicked girl!"

"She *is!*" said Mr. Goodhue, stopping, and looking down into the little eager face.

"Yes, sir, she is. She wants us to dance!"

"She *does!*"

"Yes, sir, she does. She wanted us to learn the steps, right down in her garden this afternoon. Would you dance, Mr. Goodhue?"

"Would I? Perhaps I might, were I as little and spry as you, and Winnie would teach me steps, and it was down in the garden."

The little girls looked up into his face searchingly. He walked on laughing, and they went on homeward, to ask further advice.

At home, too, everyone seemed to think it a matter for smiles, and laughed at the two tender little consciences.

So they both ran back after dinner to Mrs. Tennyson's. But on the way Kathie said, "They let us, the minister and ev'ry body, but if it is wicked *ever*, how isn't it wicked *now*?"

"I s'pose 'cause we're children," Lu said wisely.

The logical trouble thus laid, they tripped on.

They were dressed in sweet pink, and their sun-bonnets were as fresh and crisp as only the sun-bonnets of dear little country school-girls ever can be. It was a most merry summer day; all nature moving gladsomely to the full music of life. The leaves were fluttering to each other, the grasses sweeping up and down, the bobolinks hopping by the meadow path.

Their friend Winnie came out to meet them, looking rather astonished.

"We're going to learn," shouted Lu, "get on your bonnet."

"But you wasn't good to me to-day," said Winnie, thoughtfully.

"We didn't da'st to be," said Kathie, "till we'd asked somebody that knew."

Mrs. Tennyson was half of the mind to call her little daughter in; yet she felt it a pity to be less sweet and forgiving than the child.

Winnie already had her class before her. "Now you must do just as I do. You must hold your dress back so,— not grab it, but hold it back nice, and you must bend forward so, and you must point your slippers so,—not stand flat."

Very graceful the little dancing-teacher looked, tip-toeing here, gliding there, twinkling through a series of pretty steps down the long garden walk.

But the pupils! Do the best she might, sturdy little Kathie couldn't manage her dress. She grasped it tightly in either fat little fist. "Mother Bunch!" Lu giggled behind her back.

Kathie's face got very red over that. It was well enough to be "Dumpling,"—everybody loves a dumpling; but "Mother Bunch!" So she bounced and shuffled a little longer, and then she said she was going home.

But Miss Lu wasn't ready. She greatly liked the new fun, the hopping and whirling to Winnie's steady "One, two, *three!* One, two, *three!*" There was a grown-up, affected smirk on her delicate little face, at which Mrs. Tennyson laughed every time she looked out. I think Lu would have hopped and minced up and down the walk until night, if Winnie's mother hadn't told them it was time to go.

"I don't like her old steps," said Kathie. They were sitting on a daisy bank near Mr. Medway's.

"Well, I do," said Lu. "And you would, too, if you wasn't so chunked. You just bounced up and down."

Kathie burst out crying. "I'll bet dancing steps *is* wicked, for you never was so mean before in your life, so! And you didn't dance near so pretty as Winnie, and you needn't think you ever will, for you *never*will!"

"Oh! I won't, won't I?" said Lu, teasingly.

"No, you won't. I won't be wicked and say you are nice, for you're horrid."

"*You*'re wicked this minute, Kathie Dysart, for *you*'re mad."

And as she laughed a naughty laugh, and as Kathie glared back at her, then it was that that which happened began to happen. Lu's delicate, rosy mouth commenced drawing up at the corners in an ugly fashion, and her nose commenced drawing down, while her dimpled chin thrust itself out in a taunting manner; but the horror of it was that she couldn't straighten her lips, nor could she draw in her chin when she tried.

"You *dis'gree'ble* thing!" shrieked Kathie, looking at her and feeling dreadfully, her eyebrows knotting up like two little squirming snakes. "If I'm a Mother Bunch, you're a bean-pole, and you'll be an ugly old witch some day, and you'll dry up and you'll blow away."

By this time the two little pink starched sun-bonnets fairly stood on end at each other.

"Kathie Dysart, I'll tell your Sunday-school teacher, see if I don't."

"Tell her what? you old, *old*, OLD thing!"

"THEY GREW OLDER AND UGLIER EACH
MOMENT."

Kathie Dysart loved her Sunday-
school teacher, and now she *was* in a
rage. She couldn't begin to scowl as
fiercely as she felt; her cheeks sunk in,
her lips drew down, her nose grew

sharp and long in the effort. And, all at once, as the children say, her face "froze" so. Oh! it was perfectly horrid, that which happened to the two little dears, it was indeed. They could not possibly look away from each other, and they grew older and uglier each moment! Why, their very sun-bonnets—those fresh little pink sun-bonnets—shriveled into old women's caps, and even in the hearts of the poor little old crones the hardening process was going on, a fierce fire of hate scorching the last central drop of dew, until nothing would ever, ever grow and bloom again.

It was all over with Lu and Kathie forever and ever.

All this was long ago, of course—indeed, it happened "once upon a time." It would be difficult now to verify each point in the account. On the contrary, I suppose it just possible that there may be a mistake as to the transformation of the children's clothes—the change of the sun-bonnets into caps, for instance.

But, as a whole, I see no reason to doubt the story. Often, and quite recently, too, I have seen little faces in danger of a similar transformation.

Where anger, envy, spite, and some others of the ill-tempers, gain control of the nerves and muscles of the human countenance, they pull and twitch and knot and tie these nerves and muscles, until it is almost impossible to recognize the face.

Sometimes this change has passed off in a minute; but at other times it has lasted for hours, and there is *always* danger that the face will fail to recover its pleasantness wholly, that traces will remain, like wrinkles in a ribbon that has been tied, and that, at last, the transformation will be final and fatal, and the fair child become and remain "a horrid old witch."

Of one thing we all are certain—that the most gossiping and malicious person now living was once a fair and innocent child; so who shall say that this which I have related did *not* happen to Lu and Kathie?

FLAXIE FRIZZLE.

HER name was Mary Gray, but they called her Flaxie Frizzle. She had light curly hair, and a curly nose. That is, her nose curled up at the end a wee bit, just enough to make it look cunning.

What kind of a child was she?

Well, I don't want to tell; but I suppose I shall have to. She wasn't gentle and timid and sweet like you little darlings, oh, no! not like you. And Mrs. Willard, who was there visiting from Boston, said she was "dreadful."

She was always talking at the table, for one thing.

"Mamma," said she, one day, from her high chair, "your littlest one doesn't like fish; what makes you cook him?"

Mamma shook her head, but Flaxie wouldn't look at it. Mrs. Willard was saying, "When we go to ride this afternoon we can stop at the slate-quarry."

Who was going to ride? And would they take the "littlest one" too? Flaxie meant to find out.

FLAXIE FRIZZLE.

"Do you love me, mamma?" said she, beating her mug against her red waiter.

"When you are a good girl, Flaxie."

"Well, look right in my eyes, mamma. Don't you see I *are* a good girl? And *mayn't* I go a-riding?"

"Eat your dinner, Mary Gray, and don't talk."

Her mother never called her Mary Gray except when she was troublesome.

"I want to tell you sumpin, mamma," whispered she, bending forward and almost scalding herself against the teapot, "I *won't* talk; I won't talk *a*tall."

But it was of no use. Mrs. Willard was not fond of little girls, and Mrs. Gray would not take Flaxie; she must stay at home with her sister Ninny.

Now Ninny—or Julia—was almost ten years old, a dear, good, patient little girl, who bore with Flaxie's naughtiness, and hardly ever complained. But this afternoon, at four o'clock, her best friend, Eva Snow, was coming, and Ninny did hope that by that time her mamma would be at home again!

Mrs. Gray and Mrs. Willard rode off in the carriage; and the moment they were gone, Flaxie began to frisk like a wild creature.

First she ran out to the gate, and screamed to a man going by,—

"How d'ye do, Mr. Man? You *mustn't* smoke! My mamma don't like it!"

"Oh, why *did* you do that?" said Ninny, her face covered with blushes, as she darted after Flaxie, and brought her into the house.

"Well, then, show me your new picture-book, and I won't."

As long as she was looking at pictures she was out of mischief, and Ninny turned the leaves very patiently.

But soon the cat came into the room with the new kitten in her mouth, and then Flaxie screamed with terror. She thought the cat was eating it up for a mouse; but instead of that she dropped it gently on the sofa, purring, and looking at the two little girls as if to say,—

"Isn't it a nice baby?"

Flaxie thought it was; you could see that by the way she kissed it. But when she picked it up and marched about with it, the old cat mewed fearfully.

"Put it down," said Ninny. "Don't you see how bad you make its mother feel?"

"No. I's goin' to carry it over the bridge, and show it to my grandma; she wants to see this kitty."

Ninny looked troubled. She hardly dared say Flaxie must not go, for fear that would make her want to go all the more.

"What a funny spot kitty has on its face," said she, "white all over; with a yellow star on its forehead."

"Well," said Flaxie, "I'll wash it off." And away she flew to the kitchen sink.

"What are you up to now?" said Dora, the housemaid, who stood there with her bonnet on. "You'll drown that poor little creetur, and squeeze it to death too! Miss Ninny, why don't you attend to your little sister?"

Dear Ninny! as if she were not doing her best! And here it was half-past three, and Eva Snow coming at four!

"O Dodo!" said she, "you're not going off?"

"Only just round the corner, Miss Ninny. I'll be right back."

But it was a pity she should go out at all. Mrs. Gray did not suppose she would leave the house while she was gone.

As soon as "Dodo" was out of sight, Flaxie thought she could have her own way.

"O Ninny! you're my darlin' sister," said she, with a very sweet smile. "Will you lem me carry my kitty over to grandma's?"

"Why, no indeed! You mustn't go 'way over the bridge."

"Yes I mus'. 'Twon't hurt me *a* tall!"

"But I can't let you, Flaxie Frizzle; truly I can't; so don't ask me again."

Flaxie's lip curled as well as her nose.

"Poh! I haven't got so good a sister as I fought I had. Laugh to me, Ninny, and get me my pretty new hat, or I'll shut you up in the closet!"

Ninny did laugh, it was so funny to hear that speck of a child talk of punishing a big girl like her!

"Will you lem me go?" repeated Flaxie.

"No, indeed! What an idea!"

"I've got fi-ive cents, Ninny. I'll buy you anyfing what you want? Now lem me! 'Twon't hurt me *a* tall!"

Ninny shook her head, and kept shaking it; and Flaxie began to push her toward the closet door.

"*Will* you get my hat, Ninny? 'Cause when I die 'n' go to hebben, then you won't have no little sister."

"No, I will not get your hat, miss, so there!"

All this while Flaxie was pushing, and Ninny was shaking her head. The closet-door stood open, and, before Ninny thought much about it, she was inside.

"There you is!" laughed the baby.

Then rising on her "tippy-toes," Flaxie began to fumble with the key. Ninny smiled to hear her breathe so hard, but never thought the wee, wee fingers could do any harm.

At last the key, after clicking for a good while, turned round in the lock; yes, fairly turned. The door was fastened.

"Let me out! out! out!" cried Ninny, pounding with both hands.

Flaxie was perfectly delighted. She had not known till then that the door was locked, and if Ninny had been quiet she would probably have kept fumbling away till she opened it. But now she wouldn't so much as touch the key, you may be sure. O, Flaxie Frizzle was a big rogue, as big as she *could* be, and be so little! There she stood, hopping up and down, and laughing, with the blind kitty hugged close to her bosom.

"Laugh to me, Ninny!"

"What do I want to laugh for? Let me out, you naughty girl!"

"Well, *you* needn't laugh, but *I* shall. Now I's goin' to grandma's, and carry my white kitty."

"No, no, you mustn't, you mustn't!"

"*You* can't help it! I *is* a goin'!"

"Flaxie! Flax-ee!"

Oh! where was Eva Snow? Would she never come? There was a sliding-door in the wall above the middle shelf, and Ninny climbed up and pushed it back. It opened into the parlor-closet, where the china dishes stood. If she could only crawl through that sliding door she might get out by way of the parlor, if she *did* break the dishes.

But, oh dear! it wasn't half big enough. She could only put her head in, and part of one shoulder. What should she do?

It was of no use screaming to that witch of a Frizzle; but she did scream. She threatened to "whip her," and "tie her," and "box her ears," and "burn up her dollies."

But Flaxie knew she wouldn't; so she calmly pulled off her boots and put on her rubbers.

Then Ninny coaxed. She promised candy and oranges and even wedding-cake, for she forgot she hadn't a speck of wedding-cake in the world.

But, while she was still screaming, Flaxie was out of sight and hearing. She hadn't found her hat; but, with her new rubbers on her feet, and the blind kitty still hugged to her bosom, she was "going to grandma's." She ran with all her might; for what if somebody should catch her before she got there!

"The faster I hurry the quicker I can't go," said she, puffing for breath.

It was a beautiful day. The wind blew over the grass, and the grass moved in green waves; Flaxie thought it was running away like herself.

It was half a mile to the bridge. By the time she reached Mr. Pratt's store, which was half way, she thought she would stop to rest.

"'Cause he'll give me some candy," said she, and walked right into the store, though it was half full of men,— oh fie! Flaxie Frizzle!

Mr. Jones, a lame man, was sitting next the door, and she walked boldly up to him.

"Mr. *Lame* Jones, does you want to see my kitty?"

He laughed, and took it in his hands; and another man pinched its tail. Flaxie screamed out:

"You mustn't hold it by the handle, Mr. Man!"

Then they all laughed more than ever, and clapped their hands; and Mr. Jones said:

"You're a cunning baby!"

"Well," replied Flaxie, quickly, "what makes you have turn-about feet?"

This wasn't a proper thing to say, and it made Mr. Jones look sober, for he was sorry to have such feet. Mr. Pratt was afraid Flaxie would talk more about them; so he frowned at her and said:

"Good little girls don't run away bare-headed, Miss Frizzle! Is your mamma at home?"

"Guess I'll go now," said Flaxie; "some more folks will want to see my kitty."

Mr. Pratt's boy ran after her with a stick of candy, but could not catch her. She called now at all the houses along the road, ringing the bells so furiously that people rushed to the doors, afraid something dreadful had happened.

"I fought you'd want to see my kitty," said the runaway, holding up the little blind bundle; and they always laughed then; how could they help it?

But somehow nobody thought of sending her home.

When she reached the bridge she was hungry, and told the "bridge-man" she was "fond of cookies." His wife gave her a caraway-cake shaped like a leaf.

"I'm fond o' that one," said she, with her mouth full. "Please give me *two* ones."

Just fancy it! Begging food at people's houses! Yet her mamma *had* tried to teach her good manners, little as you may think it.

"I don't believe she has had any supper. It must be she is running away," said the bridge-man's wife, as Flaxie left her door. "I ought to have stopped her; but somebody will, of course."

But nobody did. People only laughed at her kitty, and then passed on.

Soon the sun set, and the new moon shone white against the blue sky. Flaxie had often seen the moon, but it looked larger and rounder than this. What ailed it now?

"Oh, I know," said she, "God has doubled it up."

She had changed her mind, and did not want to go to her grandmother's.

"Mr. Pratt fought I was bare-headed, and grandma'll fink I'm bare-headed. Guess I won't go to g'andma's, kitty, I'll go to preach-man's house; preach-man will want to see you."

On she went till she came to the church. Then she sat down on the big steps, dreadfully tired.

"Oh, my yubbers ache so! Now go s'eep, Kitty; and when you want to wake up, call me, and I'll wake you."

This was the last Flaxie remembered. When the postmaster found her, she was sitting up, fast asleep, with her little tow head against the door, and the kitty in her arms. The kitty was still alive.

Eva Snow had come and let Ninny out of the closet long ago; and lots of people had been hunting ever since for Flaxie Frizzle. When the postmaster and the minister brought her home between them, Mrs. Gray was so very glad that she laughed and cried. Still she thought Flaxie ought to be punished.

"O mamma," said Miss Frizzle next morning, very much surprised to find herself tied by the clothes-line to a knob in the bay-window. "The men laughed to me, they did! Mr. Lame Jones, he said I was very cunning!"

But for all that, her mamma did not untie her till afternoon; and then Flaxie promised "honestly," not to run away again.

Would you trust her?

FIVE POUNDS OF
CINNAMON.

hey don't name girls "Roxy," and "Polly," and "Patty," and "Sally," nowadays; but when the little miss who is my heroine was a lady, those short, funny old names were not at all old-fashioned. "Roxy," especially, was considered a very sweet name indeed. All these new names, "Eva," and "Ada," and "Sadie," and "Lillie," and the rest of the fanciful "ies" were not in vogue. Then, if a romantic, highflown young mamma wished to give her tiny girl-baby an unusually fine name, she selected such as "Sophronia," "Matilda," "Lucretia," or "Ophelia." In extreme cases, the baby could be called "Victoria Adelaide."

In this instance baby's mother was a plain, quiet woman; and she thought baby's grandmother's name was quite fine enough for baby; and so baby was called "Roxy," and, when she was ten years old, you would have thought little Roxy fully as old-fashioned as her name.

I think it is her clothes that makes her image look so funny as she rises up before me. She herself had brown hair and eyes, and a good country complexion of milk and roses—such a nice complexion, girls! You see she had plenty of bread and milk to eat; and a big chamber, big as the sitting-room down stairs, to sleep in—all windows—and her bed stood, neat and cool, in the middle of the floor; and she had to walk ever so far to get anywhere—it was a respectable little run even out to the barn for the hens' eggs; and it was half a mile to her cousin Hannah's, and it was three quarters to school, and just a mile to the very nearest stick of candy or cluster of raisins. Nuts were a little nearer; for Roxy's father had a noble butternut orchard, and it was as much a part of the regular farm-work in the fall to gather the "but'nuts" as it was to gather the apples.

Don't you see, now, why she had such a nice complexion? But if you think it don't quite account for such plump, rosy cheeks, why, then, she had to chase ever so many ways for the strawberries. Not a strawberrywas raised in common folks' gardens in those days. They grew mostly in farmers' meadows; and very angry those farmers used to be at such girls as Roxy in "strawberry time"— "strawberry time" comes before "mowing," you know—for how they did wallow and trample the grass! Besides, the raspberries and blackberries, instead of being Doolittle Blackcaps, and Kittatinnies, and tied up to nice stakes in civilized little plantations, grew away off upon steep hill-sides, and in the edges of woods, by old logs, and around stumps; and it took at least three girls, and half a day, and a lunch-basket, and torn dresses, and such clambering, and such fun, to get them!*Of course* Roxy had red cheeks, and a sweet breath, and plump, firm white flesh—*so* white wherever it wasn't browned by the sunshine.

But otherwise she certainly was old-fashioned, almost quaint. Her hair was braided tight in two long braids, crossed on her neck, and tied with a bit of black thread; there was a pair of precious little blue ribbons in the drawer for Sundays and high days. Roxy's mother would have been awfully shocked at the wavy, flowing hair of you Wide Awake girls, I assure you!

And Roxy's dress. *You* never saw a "tow and linen" dress, I dare say. Roxy's dresses were all "home-made"—not merely cut and sewed at home; but Roxy's father raised the flax in the field north of the house, and Roxy's mother spun the flax and tow into thread upon funny little wheels. Then she colored the thread, part of it indigo blue, and part of "copperas color," and after that wove it into cloth—not just enough for a dress, but enough for two dresses for Roxy, two for herself, and some for the men folks' shirts, besides yards and yards of dreadfully coarse cloth for "trousers;" and perhaps there was a fine white piece for sheets and pillowcases. Bless me! how the farmers' wives did work eighty years ago!

And how that "blue and copperas check" did wear, and how it did shine when it was freshly washed and ironed! Only it was made up so ungracefully— just a plain, full skirt, plain, straight waist, and plain straight sleeves. *You* never saw a dress made so, because children's clothes have been cut pretty and cunning for a great many years. Roxy's dresses were short, and she wore straight, full "pantalets," that came down to the tops of her shoes; for Mrs. Thomas Gildersleeve would have thought it dreadful to allow her daughter to show the shape of her round little legs, as all children do nowadays.

To finish up, Roxy wore a "tie-apron." This was simply a straight breadth of "store calico," gathered upon a band with long ends, and tied round her waist. Very important a little girl felt when allowed to leave off the high apron and don the "tie-apron."

The first day she came to school with it on, her mates would stand one side and look at her. "O, dear! you feel big—don't you?" they would say to her. Maybe she would be obliged to "associate by herself" for a day or so, until they became accustomed to the sight of the "tie-apron," or until her own good nature got the better of their envy.

A "slat sun-bonnet," made of calico and pasteboard, completed Roxy's costume on the summer morning of an eventful day in her life. It was drawn just as far on as could be. It hid her face completely. She was pacing along slowly, head bent down, to school. It was only eight o'clock. Why was Roxy so early?

Well, this morning she preferred to be away from her mother. She was "mad" at both her father and mother. "Stingy things!" she said, with a great, angry sob.

About that time of every year, June, the children were forbidden to go indiscriminately any more to the "maple sugar tub." The sweet store would begin to lessen alarmingly by that time, and the indulgent mother would begin to economize.

Every day since they "made sugar," Roxy had had the felicity of carrying a great, brown, irregular, tempting chunk of maple sugar to school. She had always divided with the girls generously. Her father did not often give her pennies to buy cinnamon, candy, raisins, and cloves with; so she used to "treat" with maple sugar in the summer, and with "but'nut meats" in the winter, in return for the "store goodies" other girls had.

For a week now she had been prohibited the sugar-tub. This morning she had asked her father for sixpence, to buy cinnamon. She had been refused. "Stingy things!" she sobbed. "They think a little girl can live without money just as well as not. O, I am so ashamed! I'd like to see how mother would like to be invited to tea by the neighbors, and never ask any of them to *her* house. I guess she'd feel mean! But they think because I am a little girl, there's no need of *my* being polite and free-hearted! Polly Stedman has given me cinnamon three times, and I *know* the girls think I'm stingy! I'm *so* ashamed!" And Roxy's red cheeks and shining brown eyes brimmed up and overflowed with tears.

Poor little Roxy! she herself had such a big sweet tooth! It was absolutely impossible for her to refuse a piece of stick cinnamon or a peppermint drop. Yesterday she had told the girls she should certainly bring maple sugar to-day. She meant to, too, even if she "took" it. But there her mother had stood at the broad shelf all the morning, making pies and ginger snaps, and the sugar-tub set under the broad shelf. There was no chance. She finally had asked her mother.

"No, Roxy; the sugar will be gone in less than a month. You children eat more sugar every year than I use in cooking. It's a wonder you have any stomachs left."

"I promised the girls some," pleaded Roxy.

"Promised the girls! You've fed these girls ever since the sugar was made. Off with you! What do you suppose your father'd say?"

Roxy wouldn't have dared tell her father. He was a stirring, hard-working man, that gave his family all the luxuries and comforts that could be "raised" on the farm; but bought few, and growled over what he did buy, and made no "store debts." It was high time, in fact, that Roxy's indulgent mother should begin to husband the sugar.

Roxy saw there would be no chance to "take" the sugar; so she had mournfully started off. Is it strange that so generous a girl would have stolen, if she could? Why, children, I have seen many a man do mean, wrong, dishonest deeds, in order to be thought generous, and a "royal good fellow," by his own particular friends; and Roxy would a thousand times rather have "stolen" than to have faced her mates empty-handed this morning. She walked on in sorrowful meditation. She thought once of going back, to see if there were eggs at the barn—she might take them down to the store, and get candy. But she remembered they were all brought in last night, and it was too early for the hens to have laid this morning.

As she pondered ways and means in her little brain, a daring thought struck her. That thought took away her breath. She turned white and cold. Then she turned burning red all over. Her little feet shook under her. But, my! What riches! What a supply to go to! How they would envy her!

"I don't care—so. They needn't be so stingy with me! And Mrs. Reub uses so much such things I don't believe it will ever be noticed in the 'account'— and, any way, it'll be six months before he settles up. Nobody will know it till then, and maybe—*maybe* I shall be dead by that time, or the world will burn up!"

With these comforting reflections, Roxy straightened up her little sun-bonneted head, doubled her little brown fists, and ran as hard as she could—and Roxy could outrun most of the boys.

On she ran, past the school-house—it was not yet unlocked—right on down to the village. She slacked up as she struck the sidewalks. She walked slower and slower, to cool her bounding pulses and burning skin.

Still her cheeks were like two blood-red roses as she walked into the cool, dark, old stone store; but for some reason, mental, moral, or physical, while her cheeks remained red, her little legs and arms grew stone cold and stiff, and spots like blood came before her eyes, and a great ringing filled her ears, as Mr. Hampshire, the merchant himself, instead of his clerk, came to wait upon her. "And what will you have, Miss Roxy—some peppermints?"

"No, sir. If you please, Mrs. Reuben Markham wants two pounds of raisins, and five pounds of cinnamon, and you are to charge it to Mr. Markham."

It was strange, but her voice never faltered after she got well begun. However, for all that, Mr. Hampshire stared at her. *"Five pounds of cinnamon*, did you say, sis?"

"Yes, sir, if you please," answered Roxy, quietly, "and two pounds of raisins."

So Mr. Hampshire went back, and weighed out the cinnamon and raisins, and gave them to her. She was a little startled at the mighty bundle five pounds of stick cinnamon made; but she took them and went out, and Mr. Hampshire went back and charged the things to Mr. Reuben Markham.

Miss Roxy went speeding back to the school-house with her aromatic bundle. Her face was fairly radiant. She had no idea five pounds of cinnamon were so much. O, *such a lot*! She had made up her mind what to do with it. She couldn't, of course, carry it home. She had no trunk that would lock, or any place safe from her mother's eyes. But in the grove, back of the school-house, there was a tree with a hollow in it. By hard running she got there before any of the scholars came. She put her fragrant packages in, first filling her pocket, and then stopped the remaining space with a couple of innocent-looking stones.

Such a happy day as it was! She found herself a perfect princess among her mates. She "treated" them royally, I assure you. Everybody was so obliging to her all day, and it was so nice to be able to make everybody pleased and grateful! Both the day of judgment and the dying day were put afar off—at least six months off.

Meantime, during the forenoon, Mr. Hampshire kept referring to the idea that any one could want *five pounds of cinnamon* at one time. Still, little Roxy was Mrs. Reub Markham's next neighbor, and it was perfectly probable that she should send by her.

Some time in the afternoon Mr. Reuben Markham came down to the store. He was a wealthy man, jolly, but quick-tempered. Mr. Hampshire and he were on excellent terms. "How are you, Markham? and what's your wife baking to-day?"

"My wife baking?"

"Yes. I concluded you were going to have something extra spicy. Five pounds of cinnamon look rather suspicious. Miss Janet's not going to step off—is she."

"I'm not in that young person's confidence. I should say not, however. But what do you mean by your five pounds of cinnamon?"

"Why, Mrs. Gildersleeve's little girl was in here this morning, and said Mrs. Markham sent for five pounds of cinnamon and two of raisins."

"Mrs. Gildersleeve's girl? I know Mrs. Markham never sent for no such things. She knew I was coming down myself this afternoon."

He followed Mr. Hampshire down the store to the desk. There it was in the day-book:—

"Reub Markham, Dr., per Roxy Gildersleeve.

To	5 pounds	cinnamon, 40c.,	$2 00
"	2 "	raisins (layer), 20c.,	40

That Mr. Reub Markham swore, must also be set down against him. He drove home in a red rage. Through the open school-house door, little Roxy Gildersleeve saw him pass; but her merry young heart boded no ill. Her mouth was tingling pungently with the fine cinnamon, and in her pocket yet were eight moist, fat, sugary raisins, to be slipped in her mouth one by one, four during the geography lesson, four during the spelling lesson.

As it happened, Mr. Gildersleeve was cultivating corn in a field that fronted the highway. He and his wealthier neighbor were not on the best of terms. A line fence and an unruly ox had made trouble. Mr. Gildersleeve had sued Mr. Markham, and beat him; and Mr. Gildersleeve didn't take any pains now to look up as he saw who was coming.

But Mr. Markham drew up his horses.

"Hello, Gildersleeve!"

"Hello yourself, Mr. Markham!"

"I say, what you sending your young uns down to the store after things, and charging them to me for? Mighty creditable that, Tom Gildersleeve!"

"Getting things and charging them to you!" Gildersleeve stopped his horse. "What do you mean, Markham?"

"You better go down and ask Hampshire. If you don't, you may get it explained in a way you won't fancy!"

He whipped up his horses and drove off, leaving Mr. Gildersleeve standing there, gazing after him as if he had lost his senses. After a moment he unhitched his horse from the cultivator, mounted him, and rode off toward the village.

School was out. Roxy had reached home. She was setting the table, and whistling like a blackbird. Things had gone so happily at school! Everything was so neat, and pleasant, and cosy at home! She saw her father ride into the yard, and go to the barn. She whistled on.

She sat in the big rocking-chair, stoning cherries, and smelling the roses by the window, when he came into the kitchen.

"Where's Roxy?" she heard him ask.

"In the other room, I guess," said mother.

He came in where she was. She looked up; and her little stained hands fell back into the pan. She knew the day of judgment had come. O, she wished it was that other day, the day of death, instead! Her mouth dropped open, the room turned dark.

Mr. Gildersleeve sank down on a chair. His child's face was too much for him. He groaned aloud. "That one of *my* children should ever be talked about as a thief! What possessed you, Roxy?"

Roxy sat before him, trembling. Not at the prospect of punishment. But she saw her father's eyes filling up with tears. "Don't, father," she said, hurriedly, trying not to cry. "I've only eaten a little, and I will carry it all back. If you will pay for what is gone, I'll sell berries or something, and pay you back the money. Mr. Hampshire is a good man; he won't tell, father, if you ask him not."

"You poor, ignorant child!"

He got up and went out, shutting the door after him. Not one word of punishment; but he left Roxy trembling with a strange terror. She shook with a presentiment of some unendurable public disgrace. Setting down the pan of cherries, she crept to the door. She heard her father's voice, her mother's sharp exclamations. Then her father said, "To think *our* girl should sin in such a high-handed way! Mother, I'd rather laid her in her grave any day!

That hot-headed Markham will not rest until he's published it from Dan to Beersheba. She's only a child, but this thing will stick to her as long as she lives."

Her mother sobbed. "Our poor Roxy! Tom, if the school children get hold of it, she will never go another day. The child is so sensitive! I don't know how to punish her as I ought. I can only think how to save her from what is before her."

O, how Roxy, standing at the key-hole, trembled to see her mother lean her head on her father's shoulder and sob, and to see tears on her father's cheeks! O, what a wicked, wicked girl! It *was* thieving; in some way it was even worse than that; as if she had committed a—a forgery, maybe, Roxy thought. She was conscious she had done something unusually daring and dreadful.

She stole off up stairs, shut herself in, and cried as hard as she could cry. Afterward her little brain began to busy itself in many directions. She tried to fancy herself shamed and pointed at, afraid to go to school, afraid to go down to the store, ashamed to go to the table, with no right to laugh, and play, and stay around near her mother, never again to dare ask her father to ride when he was going off with the horses.

So lonely and gloomy, she tried to think what it was possible to do. At last, as in the morning, a daring thought occurred to her suddenly. She made up her mind in just one minute to do it.

When her mother called, she went down to supper at once. The boys were gone. Nobody but she and father and mother; and the three had very red eyes, and said nothing, but passed things to each other in a kind, quiet way, that seemed to Roxy like folks after a funeral—perhaps it did to the rest of them. Roxy was fanciful enough to think to herself, "Yes, it is *my*funeral. We have just buried my good name."

Silently, one with a white face, the other with a red one, Roxy and her mother did up the work. Then Roxy went up to her room again. She took a sheet of foolscap, and made it into four sheets of note paper. She wrote and printed something on each sheet, and folded all the sheets into letters. Then she went down stairs. Two of the little letters she handed to her mother. Then, bonnet in hand, she stole out the front door. At the gate she looked down the road toward the village, up the road toward Mr. Markham's. She started toward Mr. Markham's. She got over the road marvelously; for the child was wild to get the thing over with. She was going up the path to the house when she saw Mr. Markham hoeing in the garden. She went to him, thrust a note into his hand, and was off like a dart.

It was a long, hard, lonely run down to the village. How lonely in the grove at the hollow tree! How like a thief, with the bundles openly on her arm! No little girl's pocket would hold them, nothing but a great Judas-bag. She went straight to the stone store. It was just sunset. How thankful she was to find nobody in the store but Mr. Hampshire himself, reading the evening paper. He looked up, and recognized the red little face. He glanced at the bundles as she threw them, with a letter, down on the counter, and whisked out through the door. He called after her, "Here, here,

Roxy; here, my dear! Come back. I have some figs for you!"

But no Roxy came back. He heard her little heels clattering down the sidewalk fast as they could go. So he got up and read the letter, for it was directed to himself.

Here are the four notes Roxy wrote:—

"Dear Father: I Will paye you every Cent if I Live. I shall always be a Good Girl, and never hanker after Only what I have Got. Please forgive Me, and Not Talk It Over with Mother. It will make her Sick.Roxy."

"Dear Mother: Please love me until I am Bad once More. If I ever, Ever, should be Bad again, then you may give me Up. Don't get Sick.Roxy."

"Mr. MarkHam: I have been Very Wicked. I have made father and Mother wretched. I am sorry. Please don't be

Hard on Me, and Set every body against me, because My Mother would settle right down and be very Sick. I am only a Little girl, and a Big Man might let me go. I have taken the Things back to the Store. Also father has Paid for them. *You* may Want something some day, and do Wrong to get it, and Then you will know How good it is.R. Gildersleeve."

"Mr. HamPshire: Please Not tell the folks that come into the Store what I did. I want a Chance to be good. If you Ever hear of my stealing again, Then you can tell, of course.R. Gildersleeve."

And here is what they said:—

Mr. Gildersleeve (crying). "Here, mother, put this away. Never speak of it to her. Poor child, I *did* mean to whip her!"

Mrs. Gildersleeve (crying). "Bless her heart, Tom, this is true repentance! Our child will not soon forget this lesson. Let us be very good to her."

Mr. Markham (laughing). "Young saucebox! But there's true grit for you! Well, I don't think I shall stoop to injure a child. Let it go. I'm quits with Tom now, and we'll begin again even."

Mr. Hampshire (laughing). "She's a nice little dot, after all. I don't see what possessed her. I'd like to show this to Maria; guess I won't, though, for it is partly *my* business to keep the little name white."

And none of them ever told. When Roxy was an old woman, she related to me the story herself. The name was kept white through life. Such a scrupulous, kindly, charitable old lady! The only strange thing about her was, that she never could eat anything flavored with cinnamon, or which had raisins in it.

The End